John's Easter Story

John 20:1–10, 19–23 for children

Written by Cynthia Agricola Hinkle
Illustrated by Len Ebert

CONCORDIA PUBLISHING HOUSE • SAINT LOUIS

I'm John. I'm on Patmos, a rocky island
Where I wrote about what I saw, touched, and heard.
God sent me to tell you of His master plan
And how, from the start, there was Jesus, the Word.

I may be an old man, now grizzled and gray,
But once I was younger and busy like you.
On the Galilee Sea I fished night and day.
Then Jesus called to me, and to Him I flew!

Long before this day, now listen as I preach,
I followed Jesus as He traveled along.
For three years, I saw Him heal people and teach
That He came to forgive and right what was wrong.

It was the first day of the Passover feast,
And Peter and I helped prepare for the meal.
The twelve of us sat, but before we could eat,
Lord Jesus surprised us when we saw Him kneel.

With a bowl of water and a linen towel,
Jesus washed all our feet of filthy road dust.
And Peter, the bold one, exclaimed with a howl—
"Now clean my hands and head, Master, if you must!"

"Except for your feet, you are clean," Jesus said.
"I want you to serve and to love as I do.
But there is one who eats a bit of My bread
Who will kick up trouble for Me; this is true."

Jesus gave each of us some bread and some wine.
He said, "Here's My body, My blood shed for thee.
Remain in Me, friends, just like grapes on a vine,
And often do this in remembrance of Me."

Others did not see the trouble among us.
But I leaned near Jesus, so I clearly saw
The Master dip bread and give it to Judas,
Who left us so quickly. (That sneaky outlaw!)

Then a few hours later, we hid in that room.
Gone was our Master, yes, gone was our dear Guide!
He had gone from us into the darkest gloom—
The enemy took Him away to be tried!

Soldiers had found Him in a garden of trees;
Torches blazed brightly as Judas kissed His face.
They grabbed our Lord. Oh, how I wanted to flee!
But I followed the Lord; with them I kept pace.

They dragged Jesus to the church and town leaders.
He spoke truth to them all; they just rolled their eyes.
He spoke truth to Pilate, who gave in to fears.
He faced the crowd, who kept yelling: "Crucify!"

At Jesus' cross I hugged Mary, His mother.
He said, "It is finished." And He bowed His head.
Then we saw from His side flow blood and water.
The worst thing had happened. Our Jesus was dead!

We grieved and we mourned; our dear Teacher was gone.
They buried Him, and we went back to our room.
Then on Sunday, Mary arrived just past dawn.
She yelled, "Come! They've taken Him out of the tomb!"

The others just stared, but Peter and I raced.
We raced out of the room. We ran right away.
We saw the stone rolled from His burial place.
(This was what we now call the first Easter day.)

Jesus came and He blessed us that very night.
"Receive the Spirit," He told us, "and forgive."
That Easter, I realized God's grace-filled might.
Jesus rose so we'll be forgiven—and live!

Dear Parents,

"In the beginning was the Word" (John 1:1).

John's Gospel is an eloquent, elegant expression of the triune God, the divinity and humanity of Christ Jesus, and of John's life as an apostle. For today's readers, this account is the source of what is often called the Gospel in a nutshell: "For God so loved the world, that He gave His only Son, that whoever believes in Him should not perish but have eternal life" (3:16). It is from John's Gospel that we have reassurance of the purpose of the Bible: "These are written so that you may believe that Jesus is the Christ, the Son of God, and that by believing you may have life in His name" (20:31). John records Jesus' words that "[the Scriptures] bear witness about Me" (5:39).

Many historians believe that John was a cousin to Jesus (his mother may have been Mary's sister), that he was a pillar of the Church, and that he died at an old age of natural causes. From the Gospels, we know that John was Jesus' closest friend. He sat next to Jesus at the Last Supper. He was the only apostle at the foot of the cross when Jesus was crucified and died, and he was among the first of them to believe that Christ had risen from the grave.

This Arch Book tells a dramatized account of John's life with Jesus and what that life means to readers today. When you read this book with your child, talk about how God called John to spread the Gospel and how God calls each of us to listen, learn, and witness just as John did.

The Editor